David O'Malley SDB

Don Bosco
Stories of Loving Kindness

Don Bosco
Publications

4

Don Bosco Publications

Thornleigh House, Sharples Park, Bolton BL1 6PQ
United Kingdom

ISBN 978-1-909080-31-7
©Don Bosco Publications, 2017

Front cover illustration reproduced by kind permission from Agustín de la Torre
www.agustindelatorre.com

Printed in Great Britain by Jump Design and Print
www.jumpdp.com

Don Bosco's life reads like an adventure story, especially when he was growing up in a family and then establishing his youth club, or Oratory, in the chaos of a rapidly expanding Turin in the mid-19th century. These stories are just a sample from many. They are offered to parents and educators as material for use in the evening in families or in assemblies and class reflections in schools.

Preface

These stories have been collected from various sources within the Salesian family. They represent some of the narratives that have circulated for many years about St John Bosco. Many of them are supported by strong historical evidence; others are part of the mythology around Don Bosco that may not have the same historical foundation.

They are offered to you as a way to get to know this great saint of the Church, the tradition that surrounds his work and the beginnings of a worldwide educational and spiritual tradition of the service of the young.

When Don Bosco put loving kindness at the heart of his way of working, he was following a long tradition. Buddhism uses the word *metta* for loving kindness. The original Judaic scripture uses the word *chesed* (pronounced hessed), and even Homer, writing in about 800BCE, used the word *agape*, which was later adopted by Christians to describe loving kindness. This cardinal virtue of the Catholic Church, often described as charity, is a natural healer, a builder of relationships and a sign of God's love alive in people. So, it is surprising that such a vital virtue is under threat in our culture and even in our family lives.

Our culture favours the rugged, independent individual, the solo hero who needs no other person. Our schools can favour such a strong focus on self-development resulting in kindness being overshadowed by personal success. The business world takes a narrow view of work, measuring the profit and loss of every action and leaving kindness in the shadows as an optional by-product of the workplace. Those who help others are often seen as 'soft'. Helping a friend in the school yard, for example, will often draw jeers before praise from other pupils. Empathy is being overwhelmed by competition or success, and kindness could become a forgotten virtue.

Just because kindness is in the shadows, it does not mean that it is absent: far from it. Our experience is full of acts of random kindness that make life worth living. Motorists breaking down on the road, people short of bus fare and those involved in accidents all witness the existence of a web of loving kindness beneath the surface of our busy lives. Here is just one example:

> At a football game between Millwall and Portsmouth, I was drunk as usual. A policewoman was ushering us fans back towards the station when she saw me staggering and went to arrest me for being drunk. Seeing that I was not disorderly, she asked if I was OK. I said: "Yes, fine, just having a good time." She said it didn't look like much fun and asked whether I drank often. I replied: "Every day," and I cried.
>
> She held my arm gently and told me to stop drinking. Life was too good to drink every day, she told me. She said I looked too good to be a drunk and was too good a man to die young. The policewoman looked at me with pity and a kindness that made me cry again and think. Two months or so later I got sober. I haven't had a drink in 17 years.[1]

---

[1] I Geddes, 'The Police Officer', in BBC Magazine, 7 January 2011, *Your Good Samaritan Stories.* Available online http://www.bbc.co.uk/news/magazine-12122809 (Accessed August 2016)

These acts of kindness sow our lives with hope, and yet they rarely make their way into the newspapers that prefer to peddle fear and disaster. Even in our conversations we tend to focus on what went wrong during the day and are less likely to name and celebrate the goodness we have received. We focus on fear, and in so doing we depart from the preventive system of Don Bosco and lose ourselves in a network of fear that Don Bosco described as the 'repressive system'. That repressive system, operating in schools, workplaces and in families, airbrushes kindness from life and leaves us all poorer as a result.

Yet psychology tells us that loving kindness activates the same parts of our brain that sex and chocolate stimulate! Not only that, kindness reduces the effects of ageing, depression and can strengthen the immune system.[2] It seems that even psychology has woken up to the benefits of loving kindness and encourages us to focus more on that part of life because, as another psychologist has suggested, being a better human can lead to the creation of a better society.[3]

So whilst being kind to others has seriously positive effects on an individual, it can also create a stronger sense of belonging and of community. The second part will only be true if we learn to focus on the positive, the kindness and the understanding that we experience each day, which means that we need to notice that kindness has been shown. Remembering the experience and perhaps talking about it later avoids us airbrushing it from our own lives. That remembering of loving kindness shifts it from below our personal radar and allows us to share it with family and community. In time we will learn to see loving

---

[2] M Babula, *Motivation, Altruism, Personality and Social Psychology: The Coming Age of Altruism* (Basingstoke: Palgrave Macmillan, 2013)
[3] S Klein, *Survival of the Nicest: How Altruism Made Us Human and Why It Pays to Get Along* [tr. D B Dollenmayer] (Melbourne: Scribe Publications, 2014)

kindness and share it more easily with others and perhaps resist the competitive fear that stalks many of our lives. Don Bosco created a space called the Oratory which was safe from the competitiveness of the streets and businesses of a chaotic area of Turin. Within the Oratory he created a home, a playground, a school and church for young people. It was a school of kindness where the young people themselves received kindness and learnt to give it in equal measure.

Today that Oratory atmosphere is needed more than ever. Every family, school and workplace can become a seedbed of loving kindness. This kindness is not for wimps—it takes courage to be kind because it makes you vulnerable. You may be laughed at or exploited or even attacked. Yet kindness challenges our individualised culture and can transform it from within. This is especially true for those who carry authority in the family, the school or the workplace. Terse, top-down instructions tend to create repression and resistance, whereas kindness creates community. With community comes energy, self-sacrifice and healing. With repression, the long-term results are resistance and fragmentation.

Don Bosco's spirituality challenges every culture to build life around loving kindness. Partly that is because it works—it brings people to life. But more importantly, Don Bosco realised from his early experience that in giving and receiving kindness he was in touch with the love that moves the world: a love that Christians call Father. Don Bosco saw this Fatherly love everywhere and in the most ordinary acts of kindness, smiles and gestures of understanding. Recognising that God was so close allowed Don Bosco to be cheerful and optimistic about even the most wayward young people.

These stories capture many aspects of that loving kindness. They will remind us of the goodness inherent in the ordinary lives of parents, teachers, youth leaders and young people. I hope that they will raise our awareness of the love of God living in people and help us to be more optimistic about ourselves and others.

David O'Malley SDB
Battersea 2016

Acknowledgements

The following books have been the main sources of inspiration for this collection of stories of Don Bosco.

Ainsworth W, SDB, *Don Bosco: The Priest, The Man, The Times,* Bolton: Don Bosco Publications, 2013

Bosco T, *Don Bosco Una Biografia Nuova,* Turin: Elledici, 1999

Chavarino J, *Smiling Don Bosco,* New York: Daughters of St Paul, 1946

Lappin P, SDB, *Stories of Don Bosco,* New Rochelle: Don Bosco Publications, 1979

Contents

INTRODUCTION:
The Importance of Stories

The tradition of a 'Salesian Goodnight' is a practice that Don Bosco took from his mother, Margaret. When she came to stay with him at the Oratory in Turin, it became part of the daily custom of that youthful community. She made sure that before they slept, each young person had a chance to calm down, let go of the day and reflect on a short positive story that helped them to sleep more peacefully. Today, the term is broadened; it may well be the first word of the day, therefore a 'Good Morning' or 'Good Morning Talk'. Don Bosco believed that the Goodnight was the "key to good moral conduct, to the good running of the house, and to success in the work of education."

These stories from the life of Don Bosco are short incidents that can be used by parents with their own children, by teachers in classroom prayers or assemblies and by youth workers in their informal education. Stories like these can help to build up the tradition of a 'Goodnight' in school, the family or youth groups where a Salesian approach is needed. Each story concludes with a focus for a brief comment afterwards, if one is needed, which will help the young person to link the story to their own life experience.

At the heart of these stories is an attitude of loving kindness that eases the tensions between people and creates a family spirit. These stories reveal the generous heart of Don Bosco and his practical living of kindness. The commitment to loving kindness by parents, teachers and youth leaders demands a lot of courage because the most loving thing to do is sometimes hard and unpopular. It is not a solo task that makes heroes but a way of life that builds deeper bonds between people. Loving kindness creates community. In these stories you will see Don Bosco's youth community, which he called the Oratory, as a constant backdrop to the kindness celebrated in each story. Notice the quality of the relationships and communication that goes on in the stories and see where the parallels lie with your own living and working alongside the young.

It is recommended that these stories are not read by the adult or the child but told by the adult after briefly reading over the tale. The point of these accounts is in the basic facts and not the details, so the adult may want to embellish the narrative with further details and make it their own story. Don Bosco himself never let the facts get in the way of a good story but never wavered in his intention to do good. Enjoy telling the stories to young people because this is the dynamic through which the human race has transmitted knowledge and values for thousands of years before writing was invented. There is something about storytelling that gives it a huge educational and moral impact as a result.

These stories are about Don Bosco and I hope that they are helpful. However, your own experience is filled with chronicles and anecdotes that have happened to you or to others that are worth telling to young people. You have a wealth of literature that can furnish a huge range of stories with a message. Become a storyteller and you will become an even more effective parent, teacher and youth worker.

TEN TIPS FOR PUTTING KINDNESS AT THE CENTRE OF YOUR LIFE

1. At the end of the day remember the good things that have happened.

2. Allow yourself to be cared for and praised by others and say 'thank you'.

3. Notice how good and patient people are around you even if they sometimes aren't kind.

4. When people start moaning, distract the focus to make it more hopeful.

5. Tell people you appreciate them and praise them often.

6. Don't let your timetable become so rigid that you can't help out a friend.

7. Forgive other people for not being perfect and trust them with a fresh start.

8. Risk being kind to someone who seems a bit scary.

9. Pray for those who are having a hard time.

10. Be gentle and kind to yourself when things go wrong.

52
Stories of Loving Kindness
from the life of
Don Bosco

1
Early Death in
Don Bosco's Family

The small farm where John Bosco was brought up had a cellar where vegetables and wine were kept cool, especially during the hot Italian summers. John's father, Francis, often went down there to work, but one summer day he developed an infection and came up from the cold cellar shaking with a fever. The fever soon developed into pneumonia. There were no antibiotics at that time and John's father died very quickly, much to the shock of everyone in the neighbourhood.

John Bosco was two years old at the time and said that his earliest memory was hearing his mother, Margaret, saying, "You have no father." The young John could not understand it at all: "Why doesn't daddy speak to me? I don't want to leave him in that room all alone!" It was only when his mother began to cry that John realised that his life had changed forever. It was this early death in the family that made John think about the importance of fathers in families. Later he made sure that he would become a father to many orphan and destitute boys in Turin.

Key Point

Sometimes the bad things that happen to us can shape positive parts of life in the future. We are not trapped by past mistakes, and we can change personal disasters into a pathway to new life.

2
Fights in the Family

John had an older brother called Joseph. Generally, they got on very well and were to become lifelong friends. However, as a young child John would occasionally take delight in winding up Joseph. When Joseph, being older and stronger, reacted in frustration, young John would lose his temper completely and a full-scale fight would begin.

On one such occasion his mother took control. She knew that it was John who had provoked the quieter Joseph to fight, and so she called John into the kitchen on his own. In the corner of the room was a rod. His mother pointed to the rod and said to John, "Bring it to me." John stood still and refused to move. "I said bring it to me," his mother repeated.

His mother had never punished any of them physically before, and John was shocked that he was going to be beaten by someone he loved very much. Was he really so bad, he thought to himself. Eventually he brought the rod to his mother. John asked her what she was going to do with it, to which she responded that he would find out soon enough.

The young John held the rod out at arm's length and his mother took it from him. John began to cry. "I know you are going to beat me now and hurt me for what I have done!" His mother asked him why she shouldn't do just that—hadn't he deserved punishment? John had no answer to that question. He realised that he was in the wrong. It was then that John looked straight at his mother and said that he was sorry and made a promise to be kinder to his brother Joseph. The rod was returned to its place.

Key Point

In punishing young people, it is vital that they know what they have done is wrong, why it is serious and that they are given a chance to put things right. There should always be the chance for a fresh start for the young, who should never be written off as they grow to maturity.

3
Admitting Mistakes

John was still only seven years old when his mother had to leave him alone at home for an hour or so from time to time. On one occasion he began to explore the house and look in places he would normally not be allowed to go. One of his main targets was a shelf on which his mother kept a bowl of fruit. In the poverty of their family, fruit like this was a rare treat. John rearranged the furniture so that he could climb up to this high shelf and get a piece of fruit. He did that successfully but in his rush to get back down, he knocked over a huge jar filled with olive oil. It smashed on the floor and John watched in horror as the oil spread across the floor and sank into the stone slabs.

This was a tragedy. Oil was very expensive and almost every meal depended on oil for cooking. He was in major trouble! He climbed down, forgetting the fruit, and started wiping up the oil. The more he rubbed the more it spread out and the smell of the oil filled the whole house. There was no covering up this disaster for John. His mother would be blazing mad and he would be punished as never before. Then he got an idea. He finished the cleaning up as best he could and replaced the fruit and the furniture. Then he picked up the rod from the corner of the kitchen and went out to meet his mother before she got home.

He met his mother and offered to help carry one of the baskets she had brought from the village. His mother was delighted to see him and they chatted for a while as they walked. Eventually she asked him if everything was fine at home. John didn't say anything but instead offered her the rod he had brought from the kitchen and told her she would really have to beat him hard this time. "What have you done now?" his mother cried. So John explained. In the process of describing how he tried to clean up while slipping around the oily floor, his mother began to laugh out loud. She never used the rod on John because he confessed to his bad behaviour straight away—and also because he had made her laugh after a tiring day of shopping.

Key Point

Honesty is always the best policy because it keeps the trust between people healthy and strong. Often it removes the need for severe punishments and turns mistakes into a chance to learn and to deepen friendships.

4
Climbing Trees—Getting Stuck

John Bosco grew up in the countryside and knew his way around the fields and woods of his local area. He became a great climber of trees. He always looked at a tree to work out how best to climb it and how high he could get. As he got older he got more confident and also became interested in the nests he found up in the higher branches of the trees. Many boys of his age also caught and kept birds in cages as pets, and John was keen to catch a nightingale that he knew would sing and entertain his friends.

He was climbing a tree one day when he saw a nest that he thought was a nightingale's nest and, because it was higher and more difficult to reach, he struggled to get to it safely. As it was getting late, he climbed down and went home knowing he could come back later in the week. When he returned, however, he found the nightingale and all its chicks were dead on the ground. He was upset but decided to climb up to see what had happened. As he got closer he saw that a large magpie had taken over the nest after killing the nightingale family. He decided that he would take one of the magpie chicks instead and started to edge towards the nest. To do so he had to jam his arm into a gap between two branches. He scared the magpie off and leaned out to touch the nest. It was then he realised that his arm was stuck. He couldn't move. He tried to free his arm but it just became more wedged in the branches. Then his arm began to bruise and swell up so that he was unable to move in any direction.

It was impossible. The tree was well away from his home, and it was getting dark. He began to call out for his mother or anyone who was near. Eventually his mother, wondering where he was, had started to search for him and heard his shouts. She could do nothing to help him so asked the neighbours for help. Two of them brought a ladder out and, once they had climbed the tree, they realised they would need to go back and get a saw. They cut off one of the branches thus releasing John's arm, which was bruised for many weeks afterwards.

Key Point

Sometimes, as young people grow, they can get into situations that they can't get out of. Their apparent confidence collapses and they become dependent again. Despite all their apparent independence, they still need adults to guide and protect them as they learn the hard lessons of experience.

5
Being Robbed—Knowing the Value of Things

John and Joseph were expected to work at home and help with family chores. One of those jobs was taking the turkeys around different parts of the farm to fatten them up for market. They were doing that when a stranger leaned over the hedge and commented on what wonderfully fat turkeys they had. The boys both agreed and were proud that they had helped to rear such fine cooking birds. With a big smile on his face, the stranger admired the turkeys and told them that they would bring in a lot of money at the market. The stranger asked how much they might cost. The boys had no real idea because they had not yet taken them to market.

"Do you know," said the stranger, "for a really fat turkey I would be ready to pay as much as fifty five centesimi."[4] He said it slowly and the boys felt sure that it must be a lot of money. They agreed to sell him one, and he chose the fattest. Then he counted the money into John's hand being careful to use only small coins that eventually filled John's hands. Full of excitement they brought the remaining turkeys home and handed the money to their mother. "We sold a turkey for you!" they both said together. Margaret asked how much they had been paid. John extended his hands and said proudly, "Fifty five centesimi!"

---

[4] A *centesimo*, plural *centesimi*, was 1/100th of an Italian lira, the currency of Italy before the introduction of the euro on 1 January 1999

Their mother's face fell and she told them that they had been robbed. The turkey was worth many times that price. The boys were so sad and angry. They both ran off to find the man who had taken the turkey but he had disappeared into thin air.

Key Point

If you don't know the real value of something, you are likely to give it away too cheaply. That applies to friendship and trust between friends as well as the time and money that parents spend on their children.

6
Kindness and Sharing

John had a friend close to his own age with whom he spent a lot of time as they both had to take their milking cows out to graze. His name was Secondo and they used to talk and whittle wood into all sorts of shapes to keep from being bored. Each day they would bring a simple packed lunch with them. Secondo's family gave him poor black bread which was hard and tasteless. John was usually given softer and tastier white bread. They talked about the bread and eventually John said, "Shall we swop our bread?" Secondo was a bit confused, "You want to swap your nice soft bread for my hard black bread?" John said that he actually liked the black bread and he convinced Secondo to make the swop every day that they met up to graze their cattle.

It was only years later that Secondo realised that John was being kind to him so that he could eat better. On John's part it was a sign that, even as a young boy, he was generous and had an inner strength. He was able to sacrifice things for the good of others.

Key Point

Being able to think of others and put them first is one way to build up friendships and the inner strength to do the right thing. Do it in little things and you will have the courage later to do even greater things.

7
Dealing with Poltergeists—Courage

During the time when the grapes were being harvested, many farmers asked for help from their family and neighbours so that the grapes could be collected when they were at their best. So John walked with his family the many miles to his grandfather's farm to help with the harvest. In the evening, around the table, the family began to tell ghost stories. Everyone seemed to have a story to tell and they all laughed, if a little nervously, about the weird stories they were hearing.

But they stopped laughing when they heard noises from the loft above. Everyone was at the table; no-one was missing! Some of the family began to get nervous. They thought it could be the wind, but there was no wind. They thought it was just their imagination, but they all had heard it. The fear built up as they listened to the noises from a loft that they knew was empty and locked. John's mother suggested they leave the house which was obviously haunted. Most agreed and were leaving when John said, "I want to see what it is," and, despite many protests, he climbed the ladder up to the locked loft. As he got closer to the loft door, the noises got louder and there was banging on the roof and on the floor.

Someone passed John a lantern and he unlocked the loft door and climbed in. For a while there was silence and then even more banging. Some others climbed in with another lantern and they all saw an object moving across the loft all by itself. If they shouted, it stopped, and when they went quiet, it moved. John crept up to the object—a kind of tub with a sieve at one end. They told John not to touch it, saying it was cursed. But very quickly John lifted the lid and stepped back. Then everyone laughed with relief because under the tub was a hen. It had been trying to pick at the seeds left in the sieve when it fell over and trapped the chicken.

Key Point

Sometimes it's easy to be persuaded by other people to do something or avoid something or someone. It takes courage to think for yourself and to make your own judgements.

8
Not by Fists but by Loving Kindness—Self-Control

John had an older half-brother called Anthony who had to take all the responsibility for the farm when John's father died. He didn't like the idea of John doing part-time study. "Why should poor people like us need to study?" he argued. It used to make him angry when John took his lunch break in the fields on his own, trying to read and do his homework. It came to a head one evening when Anthony picked up John's books and tried to throw them on the fire. "I am fit and strong enough to work and I never looked at a book in my life!" he shouted at John. John told him that there was a donkey in the next field that had bigger muscles than he had. Then John ran to escape a good beating from his older brother.

These fights became more frequent as John grew older. It was tearing the family apart. So it was with a sad heart that Margaret took John aside and asked him to leave the home. She asked him to go to a neighbouring farm where he could work and pay his own way. He was only a young teenager as he set out for a local farm where he was given work for a few months, but then he was asked to leave when the work dried up. He then moved on to his last hope—some distant relatives who were quite prosperous. When he arrived he asked for a job, but the farmer told him to go and find work elsewhere. John was tired and shocked. He just sat down in the dirt and refused to move. He was destitute at such a young age. Eventually he began to cry; he was homeless, homesick, hungry and abandoned. In due course, the farmer reluctantly gave in under pressure from his wife, and John survived that winter.

Key Point

We all have our limits and in the end we have to rely on other people. John grew up with a stubborn streak and a tendency to wind people up—he had to build up his self-control if he was to get along with others.

9

A Wisdom Figure in Don Bosco's Early Life

John Bosco was lucky to find a wise guide as he was growing up. He was a local parish priest called Fr Calosso. John met him while running back to his home from Mass. The priest shouted a friendly hello and John stopped. Priests didn't usually talk to young people but Fr Calosso seemed different. Hearing that John had been to Mass, Fr Calosso asked John what the sermon was about. To the priest's amazement John repeated the whole sermon word for word. "Who are you?" asked Fr Calosso. Hearing that he was Margaret's boy, he dropped in to see the family and soon arranged for John to come to him for lessons so that his obvious talent could be developed.

John was delighted and he very quickly learnt a lot about writing, history, Latin and scripture. Things seemed to be looking up for John at last. But then Fr Calosso became terminally ill and he could not give any more lessons. However, he did tell John in public that when he died he wanted John to have all his money to help with his studies. He gave him a key and pointed to a cupboard saying that the money in there was for him. All too soon Fr Calosso died and his relatives came to mourn. There was a lot of talk about Fr Calosso's money, and John was so upset about losing his friend and guide that he could not stand the money arguments. After a few hours he gave the key to Fr

Calosso's nephew saying that he did not want to be the cause of any family arguments at such a sad time.

Key Point

We all need wise people in our lives. People we can trust and who can teach us in a friendly and safe way about life. Some people come into and out of our lives very quickly and leave us changed. Who has been your wise guide? Who has left you changed?

10
Keeping Busy and Doing New Things

John Bosco was from a very poor family. There was little extra money after the food was bought. Even clothes were handed down or shared with the neighbours. John started to devise ways to make a little pocket money. He taught himself to weave straw hats in different sizes and was able to sell them for a few coins at the local market. Then he developed this skill into making baskets, which yielded a higher price, sometimes filling them with mushrooms he had collected early in the morning before the market. Later he realised that if he could make a basket, he could make a birdcage and put something in it. He trapped birds such as nightingales and took them in a cage to the market and made a good profit. With the money, he was able to buy and make things to use in his acrobatic and magic shows.

Key Point

John was always busy, using his imagination and trying new ways of doing things. He kept busy with his hobbies and his studies and this helped him to keep cheerful and optimistic about his plans.

11
Practise the Skills You Want to Develop

The end of August always meant fairs and carnivals in John's neighbourhood. These were the last celebrations before school began again. John had been watching the circus performers for years and had practised many of their tricks back home at the farm. But this particular year he saw something new. The acrobat had put up a pole that was about 25 feet high (7.62 metres). On top was a cartwheel from which hung a large piece of ham, a huge chunk of cheese and a bag of money. He watched the acrobat climb the pole and carefully cover all of the pole with grease to make it slippery.

Then the acrobat challenged anyone to pay a small fee and climb the pole to bring down a prize to take away. Soon a crowd of farmers took up the challenge but they failed. One by one they got three quarters of the way up before their grip weakened and they slid down. John watched almost a dozen people try before he noticed that none of them took a rest on the way up. So he offered his money and began to climb. About a quarter of the way up John leaned on his heels and lowered his arms to have a rest. The crowd below jeered and laughed, thinking he had given up. But the laughter turned to cheering as he closed the distance to the prizes on the cartwheel above his head. He reached out and unhooked the cheese and ham, dropping them to the crowd below. The money bag he tucked inside his shirt and carefully climbed down into a sea of applause.

Key Point

If we want something badly, we often have to pace ourselves and not expect to be successful all at once. John was thoughtful; he watched before he acted and broke down the challenge into easier and smaller parts.

12
Hang on to Good Memories

John Bosco eventually got to school much later than other boys of his age, so he was put into a class of young lads. He hated it but decided to study so hard that he would be able to move up a class very quickly. However, he still had farm work to do and was often busy early in the morning, so, occasionally, he would forget to bring the right books. He was in trouble with the strictest teacher in school one day because instead of bringing his Latin book with him, he had brought a grammar book by mistake. The boys around him saw that he had the wrong book and were delighted when the teacher asked John to read the day's Latin passage and translate it. They all waited for the teacher to fly into a rage at John. But John held up his grammar book and recited the Latin passage word perfectly and then translated it accurately. The whole class applauded and the teacher, not knowing what John had done, lost his temper. He only calmed down when he took the grammar book from John and examined it carefully. He was amazed and told John to use his gift of a photographic memory positively and for the good of others.

Key Point

We all have the ability to remember, to think back and call to mind something in the past. If we remember good things, our mood can change and we can be more cheerful. If we remember tough times, we can learn from our past. However, if we only remember the bad things that have happened, it can make us miserable. So be careful about how you use your memory.

13
John Bosco's Dog—Learning to Let Go

As a boy John Bosco had a dog, a beagle called Polacco. He taught it to do tricks like climbing ladders and jumping onto the backs of cows when John was looking after the cattle. He even taught it to carry his coat on its back for miles when the weather was hot. They were inseparable. So it was with great sadness that he gave Polacco away to distant family members who needed it to hunt rabbits so that they could put more food on the table. With a heavy heart, John took Polacco the five or so miles to his relatives and left it with them. He reached home and sat down wearily at the table and almost immediately felt the familiar fur of Polacco at his feet. Later the relatives came back and took the dog away. Within a few hours it was back again with John. After three attempts the relatives gave up and John kept the dog at home.

Key Point

It is important to appreciate pets, family and friends, but you have also got to allow them to be free. If you cling to pets or to people too tightly, you can suffocate them with kindness. Most of all, don't cling too firmly to things or they will take over your life. Always be ready to let go.

14
Knowing When to Stop

John Bosco was a clever practical joker. As a young student in a hostel in town he gave the warden a hard time. On one particular day the warden had cooked a full chicken for the students seated round the table. However, when he took the lid off the pot, a live chicken jumped out and wrecked the kitchen as it fluttered around. Another time John asked the warden where his keys were and, finding them missing, he searched everywhere. Eventually John pointed to the pot of soup where he fished out his keys dripping with mushroom soup.

This was all fun for John, but it worried the warden who could not see how he was doing these things. He believed John was using black magic, and he reported John to the monsignor in charge of the college. John was called to see the monsignor and got off to a bad start by stealing his purse and watch then hiding them under a lampshade. The monsignor was really angry with him until he explained how he had done it. Then John showed him half a dozen other tricks and taught him one or two to use on the other priests. They both parted company happy and smiling.

Key Point

It's OK to have fun and enjoy a trick or two on others, but it can turn sour if you do it too much. As soon as you know that people are upset and you still keep teasing or gossiping, you are in the wrong. You end up doing something that deliberately upsets others and could turn you into a bully.

15
Managing Anger

One morning there was new lad in the class. He seemed quiet and shy and didn't join in any games. One of the bigger lads challenged him to join in a game, but the quiet lad shook his head. That seemed to annoy the bigger lad who then swore at him. When there was no response, he gave the newcomer a slap round the face. At that point John Bosco got angry at the treatment the new boy was getting. He told them all to leave him alone and a fight began. John picked up the bigger of the lads and swung him like a battering ram into the whole group so that they all fell to the floor.

That was when the teacher walked in. Listening to what had happened, he marvelled at John's strength and warned them all to calm down. No punishment was given on that occasion. In break time after class, John approached the new boy and introduced himself, expecting some thanks for defending him in class. Instead the new boy, Comollo by name, told him off for losing his temper and acting out of anger with such violence. John was surprised by that reaction, but he was also interested in the way that Comollo was thinking. He was different, definitely not a wimp but quietly strong. John decided that Comollo had a lot to teach him and so they became the best of friends.

Key Point

Acting out when we are angry rarely does much good. We usually end up hurting others and disappointing ourselves. Letting your anger flare up too often can lead to violence in words and actions that can make you into an unthinking animal for short periods of time. You end up out of control.

16
The Importance of Praise and Encouragement

John was taking a hiking trip for the day with some teenage friends. They had arranged to have a meal at a local parish house, but as they got near to the parish they heard that the priest was away all day. They would get no meal—he had forgotten about their visit! John asked a few neighbours if there was anyone at the priest's house. They told him there was a dragon of a housekeeper called Madalena who kept everything organised and locked up, threw nothing away and was the most miserable person to deal with.

The group elected John as their spokesperson and, having nothing to lose, he knocked on the parish house door. Madalena appeared at the door and said immediately, "The priest is out!" and began to shut the door. John explained that they were all friends of the priest. "Well, he's still out!" replied Madalena.

"In that case may I speak to Miss Madalena?" enquired John. "Why would you want to see her?" the housekeeper replied. John said, "Madalena is famous in the area for being efficient and organised, someone who could save food and make a meal out of leftovers like no-one else. Without her," John added, "people think the whole parish would be in chaos. So it's a shame that she is not here for us to meet."

At that point Madalena introduced herself and made sure the group had a good meal and even opened up the wine cellar for the lads to have a drink.

Key Point

If you can find something good to say about someone and praise them for what they do, you are more likely to see the best of them. Criticising others usually makes them cold and defensive, and it destroys the trust that could lead to friendship.

17
What Goes Around Comes Around

As a young priest Don Bosco had to make a journey to a distant parish church. He decided to hire a horse for the day because he was quite a good rider. He set off at a good pace and was over halfway there when a flock of birds suddenly rose from a field and scared the horse. It bolted and jumped the hedge into another field and was out of control. The horse's harness eventually snapped and Don Bosco was thrown into the air and landed unconscious on a pile of stones. But he was lucky. A local farmer had seen the accident and came along with his wife and took him to the farm, collecting his horse and saddle along the way. The Brina family called a doctor and insisted that John stay the night. Don Bosco was full of thanks, but the farmer said it didn't matter, explaining that he had travelled a lot and often had to be helped by strangers when he was away from home.

Don Bosco asked him to recount some of the stories of his own travel problems. Mr Brina told him of a time when he fell with his horse into a ditch. He couldn't get the horse out. It was winter, cold and wet and in the middle of nowhere. Even though it was past midnight, Mr Brina started to shout for help with little hope of being heard. So he was surprised that five minutes later he saw lanterns coming towards him across the fields. He was helped to pull the horse out of the ditch, given a hot meal and offered the best bed in the house. The next day he told the generous family that he would like to pay something for their kindness. They refused, but one of them, a student priest, said that he should do something good for anyone else in trouble in the future. So Mr Brina and his family had been doing that happily ever since.

Don Bosco raised his head from his pillow with surprise on his face. "What was the name of the family that helped you?" he asked. "They were called Bosco, and that student priest was right about doing good for others. I'll bet he made a very good priest," Mr Brina replied. Don Bosco smiled and said, "I hope he's a good priest too because you're talking to him right now."

Key Point

Doing good and being generous sets up waves of goodness that go out into people's lives. One small good act can ripple out and do good for years into the future.

18
Protecting Others by
Your Presence

When Don Bosco was in year 9, one of his teachers was so pleased with the class that he invited them all to a picnic to celebrate. With his own money he provided the food, and they hiked into the countryside to a well-known park where they could play some amazing games away from the noise and pollution of Turin. Walking back, the teacher, Fr Banaudi, met an old friend and they decided to stop a few miles before Turin to chat in a bar. He dismissed the boys and, as far as he was concerned, the outing was over.

On the way back the group passed The Red Fountain, a spring that crashed into the river bed and created a natural pool. Being hot and after a tiring day, some of the boys were tempted by the cool water and decided to swim. This split the group because some wanted to get home and others wanted to prolong the day with a refreshing dip in the water. The first one in was a boy called Philip. He dived into the cool water to the cheers of his friends. They waited for him to emerge. With mounting fear, they waited longer and longer. They shouted for him, thinking that he might be out of the water and hiding somewhere, but there was only silence. When help arrived it took over an hour to find Philip's body. The memory of that accident stayed with the young John Bosco as a reminder of the importance of adult presence and guidance for young people. He was always sure that Philip would not have drowned if his teacher had been there.

Key Point

Being there is vital in many ways when taking care of each other. Without a friendly presence or word of guidance, young people often miss the obvious consequences of their actions.

19
Fighting Boredom

Don Bosco was on his way to say an extra Mass in a parish near the centre of Turin. He sat at the back of the church to pray quietly before he said the Mass. It was then that he noticed someone snoring. He looked around and saw a group of lads sat along the wall at the very back of the church. All of them were asleep. Don Bosco crouched down and gave one of them a shake. He asked his name and the lad told him he was called Charlie and was from Lombardy, a good distance from Turin, and that he was a bricklayer's apprentice. "What are you doing here?" Don Bosco asked.

"We came in for Mass like we do at home, but the whole thing was so boring that we all gave up and decided to doze off. I didn't even know the Mass had ended Father!" Don Bosco smiled and said he understood. Then he gave Charlie the address of his Sunday Club and promised that he would be able to understand every word of any Masses that they celebrated and they would never fall asleep during a Don Bosco Mass.

Charlie came along on Sunday and brought a few of his apprentice friends. Week by week he brought more until there were a huge number of young apprentices among Don Bosco's boys.

Key Point

The Gospel is basically very simple and doesn't need to be too complicated. Adults can overcomplicate the Gospel and need to simplify its message for young people.

20
Learning by Doing

Early one morning Don Bosco went into the city to visit the barber's. He needed a shave, so he went to the usual place and found that a new apprentice had been employed. He was sweeping the floor, and Don Bosco smiled at him as he sat down to wait. The barber said he would be with him in a few minutes but Don Bosco said he would like the new apprentice to shave him.

The barber was shocked, stating, "He hasn't been trained yet; he only knows how to put the soap on." Don Bosco said that the apprentice had to learn sometime so he may as well practise on him. The barber protested, "Don Bosco! That boy couldn't shave a coconut! But if you want to be a martyr, go ahead."

So the apprentice, Charles Castini, approached Don Bosco with the open razor trembling in his young shaking hands. Don Bosco put a reassuring hand on Charles' arm, saying, "As long as you don't cut my throat Charles, this will be a great success!" The barber turned his back—he couldn't watch. Eventually Charles finished, and during that time the barber had shaved three other people. But he did a reasonable job, and there were only three or four small cuts where Don Bosco was still bleeding. Don Bosco left him a generous tip and said, "Now your apprenticeship has really begun!"

Key Point

Young people learn most things by doing, through experience and then reflection. They need to be trusted with responsibility in a supported way if they are to grow in skill and in maturity.

21
Favouritism

Don Bosco was walking through Turin to attend a meeting with the archbishop. He was called over by a shoeshine boy who offered to polish his shoes for free. Don Bosco said he was in a big rush and needed to keep going. Just then another of Don Bosco's youth club lads ran up with his shoeshine kit and offered to shine his shoes as well. The first boy was annoyed and pushed him away. A fight started about which of them was the better friend of Don Bosco. After Don Bosco separated them and calmed them down, they still wanted an answer—which of them did Don Bosco like the best?

The two boys sat expectantly waiting for the answer. Don Bosco said it was a really hard question to answer, then he held up his hand. "You see this finger and this thumb?" he said showing them his right hand. They nodded. "Which do you think I like the most?" Don Bosco asked. The boys agreed that he would like them both equally. "And that's how I like you—equally!" Don Bosco explained. Then he encouraged them to be friends and went on his way to see the archbishop.

Key Point

Favouritism always leads to jealousy and resentment. Everyone needs to be treated fairly even if we feel more comfortable with some people than with others.

22
Living a Balanced Life

Don Bosco was doing something new in Turin. He set up his Sunday Club which attracted hundreds of young people. They were often rowdy and their games and noise frightened local neighbours. He also said lively and youth-friendly Masses for them which annoyed some of the local parish priests. He was also working very hard, he was overtired and in debt for long periods of time. For that reason, some of the local priests decided that Don Bosco had become insane and needed to be locked away in a mental health facility. Partly this was out of care for him, a misunderstanding of his work and, perhaps, out of jealousy of his successful work with young people.

The local priest made a plan to abduct Don Bosco and have him locked up. Two priests arrived with a carriage and left it outside while they spoke to Don Bosco. Their plan was to lock him in the carriage and then take him to the asylum. They sat with Don Bosco and shared a drink with him and, as he relaxed, they then suggested that they all go for a ride in the country to get some fresh air away from Turin.

To their surprise, Don Bosco agreed that it was a good idea and went to get his coat. The two priests smiled at each other in silence. This was going very well. When they got to the carriage they asked Don Bosco to get in but he insisted they went first. Once they were in the locked carriage Don Bosco hit the side of the carriage hard and shouted to the driver, "To the mental hospital as quick as you can!" The driver shot off along the road with the two priests banging and shouting inside the locked carriage. The driver ignored them assuming they were patients, as did the nurses at the hospital. It took until late evening for them to convince people that they were sane. In the process Don Bosco proved he was far saner than many of the priests of Turin.

Key Point

Don Bosco is not a great example of living a balanced life. He often worked himself close to burnout and had to take time off when he became ill through overwork. Most of us have to find a healthy mix of work, rest, prayer and friendships if we are to be at our best and ready to help others. "All work and no play makes Jack a dull boy," as the old saying goes.

23
Make the First Move in Building Friendship

Don Bosco was walking down the street one warm afternoon when he passed a group of lads gambling on the pavement. They had a pack of cards and a pile of money between them. Don Bosco approached the group and asked if he could join them. The boys were suspicious; why should a priest want to join their card game? As far as they knew, priests were against card games. Don Bosco said he had the money to put in—why should it matter if he were a priest or not? So the boys let him join in.

During the game Don Bosco learnt all their names, he found out what they did and where they lived, if indeed they lived anywhere. He was getting relaxed with the boys until he began to win almost every round of the game. The boys were getting frustrated, and the pile of money in front of Don Bosco was growing bigger and bigger. Eventually he cleaned them out of all their money and stood to go. The boys looked upset to have lost all their money but Don Bosco said, "I'll tell you what I'll do. If you come to my Sunday Club, I will give you all your money back. What do you say?" The boys were delighted to make such an easy promise to get their money back, and they turned up on Sunday and quickly got to know the Salesian way of doing things.

Key Point

If you want to get to know people and get along with them, make the first move in saying hello and be interested in what interests them. Don't talk too much about yourself or your ideas but focus on the goodness of the other person and you will have good friends.

24
Persevering

Don Bosco had been running his Sunday Club for a few years but every few months the neighbours complained about the noise. When he used a parish centre, the parishioners complained about noise or the damage incurred. Each Sunday Don Bosco had to tell the boys where they were going to meet the following week, and as the numbers were increasing every week, it was starting to be impossible to organise.

One Sunday, after eighteen months of moving around like this, Don Bosco was ready to give up. He asked the lads to pray because next week, for the first time, he had nowhere to meet them. He was telling the boys all this bad news when a man walked across the open field where they were meeting and asked for Don Bosco. "I believe you're looking for a place for the lads to meet," he said. He then went on to describe a place he had available. The whole group followed the man, whose name was Mr Pinardi, and they saw what was on offer. When Mr Pinardi realised that Don Bosco wanted this space for meeting with poor boys and establishing a church for them, he became enthusiastic about the project. He added a stretch of field, offered to lay a new floor in the building and build up some of the walls. They made a deal there and then on the condition that the Pinardi family could join them for Mass every Sunday.

Key Point

Sometimes you have to struggle for quite a while before things start to work for you. It could be learning a lesson, playing sport, practising a musical instrument or trying to control your temper. It's only by keeping going and persevering that things eventually fall into place and help arrives. But if you give up too soon, you will never know what you might have achieved.

25
Accentuate the Positive

On Sundays Don Bosco sent a few lads out on the streets in Turin ringing a bell to remind young people to come to his club that he called the Oratory. It was a great way to gather the boys and they filled the streets on the road to the Oratory. Most people were happy with that arrangement but some were not happy at all. They were the parish priests who thought that these boys should be going to their own parish churches rather than to Don Bosco. They regularly complained to one another about these boys.

One of Don Bosco's staff members was a priest called Fr Borel, and he tried to argue the case for Don Bosco. He pointed out to them that most of the boys had never seen the inside of a church since they were baptised, most of them didn't have a parish and couldn't tell you which parish they might belong to. He reminded them that the Sunday Mass was designed for adults and was difficult for the uneducated youth to understand. When they went to the Oratory they built up good friendships, learnt about the Gospel and attended Mass and Confession in a youth-friendly way. "If you are patient," Fr Borel said, "these lads will grow up into good Christians and honest citizens." Most of the priests recognised the truth of Fr Borel's words but a few continued to complain about Don Bosco for years.

Key Point

Sometimes, "the better is the enemy of the good," as Don Bosco often said. You could also say that if a thing is really good to do, it is sometimes worth doing it badly. It is easy to pick holes in the work that others do and criticise them. That usually produces resentment and robs people of the energy to do the good that they can. Therefore, give praise to people for the good they do and don't overstress their flaws.

26
Trust in the Goodness of Others

Don Bosco was walking home late at night from a sick call when he found his way blocked by five or six young men. He wanted to run in the other direction but decided to put on a friendly face to them. "How's it going lads?" he asked. One of them replied, "Not so good, not good at all. We don't have any money and the pubs are closing soon. A good priest like you should give us the price of a drink." Don Bosco replied, "I'd be delighted to buy you all a drink lads but on one condition." The lads were suspicious. "What's your condition?" their leader asked. "That I have a drink with you," said Don Bosco. "No problem with that at all. Any more conditions?" their leader asked. "Maybe," said Don Bosco, "but later. Let's get that drink first."

At the bar their leader raised his glass and spoke to the whole pub. "Let's raise our glasses to Don Bosco, the best priest in the whole city of Turin!" When they were all relaxed and happy, Don Bosco invited them to come to his Sunday Club (or Oratory). Then he said they should all get home as it was now very late. "Home?" said their leader. "None of us have a home to go to!" To which Don Bosco replied, "In that case you'd better come home with me." They were delighted with the idea but Don Bosco's mother was not so pleased. They had to turn their home upside down and borrow from neighbours to find enough bedding. They eventually got settled and went to sleep in a loft space. In the morning Don Bosco went to wake them but found them gone, along with all the bedding they had used. That was a serious expense at the time, and they could not afford to lose money in replacing the bedding. "What will you do now?" His mother asked. "Keep trying," replied Don Bosco.

Key Point

Beginning anything can be very difficult. Few people get things right the first time. If we focus on what went wrong and become frustrated, we will not have the heart to try again. Instead, focus on the good points and you will find the energy to keep improving. Try to surround yourself with encouraging friends.

27
Hospitality for the Weak and Needy

It was a wild winter's night as Don Bosco and his mother were at home getting the best of the heat from a dying fire. There was a tap at the door. It wasn't loud but it was persistent. Both Don Bosco and his mother assumed it was someone who wanted a sick call from a priest. Instead, when Don Bosco opened the door, there was a lone boy standing in the dark. He was soaked to the skin and wearing clothes many sizes too big for him. "People said you would give me a place out of the rain," the boy said. Margaret took him by the arm and led him inside quickly and closed the door before the heat was lost from the room. "God preserve us!" she exclaimed. "Get those clothes off and dried by the fire. Put this blanket around you and warm yourself up!"

Within a short time he was huddled in a warm blanket with his feet tucked into one of Don Bosco's slippers. As he was eating his first hot meal for weeks, he told them his story. He was from the countryside and, despite being only 11 years old, he had come to Turin to look for work. He came to the town because both his parents had died from influenza during autumn. But he hadn't found work and was now starving and homeless. With a glance at his mother, Don Bosco left to find some sheets and a straw mattress and made up a bed near the fire. Margaret tucked the lad into his bed and then said a prayer and told him a story that made him relaxed and hopeful despite his terrible problems. The boy, whose name was never recorded, was the first young person to stay in a Salesian house. He didn't run away and stayed with Don Bosco through the winter. Don Bosco found him an apprenticeship and he went back to his home area in late spring. This experience started the custom of saying a few cheerful words and a prayer with young people each night. It is one that is continued in every Salesian house to this day, and in Salesian schools it is often part of the morning assembly.

Key Point

The last words you say to a person at the end of a conversation, at the end of a day or when they are going away are important. They can leave a person in a positive or negative mood. Don Bosco was always keen to leave people feeling good about themselves even if he had to tell them off. He always left them with a sense of hope.

28
Eating in the Dark and Thoughtlessness

Don Bosco was constantly in demand around the city of Turin, and sometimes he forgot to eat anything for the whole day. His mother often left some food in the kitchen at night so he could always have something when he came home. One night he came home very late and he was starving. Because everyone else was asleep, he didn't want to light any candles so he found the food on the table and ate it in the dark. The next morning one of the apprentices who was having breakfast with the other boys said to Don Bosco, "Where is the glue I left here for today's bookbinding work?" No-one knew where it had gone until Don Bosco remembered the funny taste of the soup he had eaten in the dark the night before. Then, with embarrassment, Don Bosco owned up to eating it by mistake. At first the boys thought he was joking with them but then they began to laugh until they cried.

Key Point

Sometimes we can all do thoughtless things, especially when we are tired. It is easy to make mistakes. When things go wrong it is usually through thoughtlessness rather than people being hurtful. It is usually better to assume a person has made a mistake through thoughtlessness than to assume they want to harm you.

29
The Consequences
of One's Actions

The political situation in Turin was very unstable during the early years of the Oratory. Many of the older boys were being recruited into various local militia groups to be controlled by unscrupulous adults for political purposes. One of the ways that Don Bosco distracted them from this temptation was to run his own 'war games' at the Oratory. They had some fairly rough games based on battles, which served to dampen the romantic ideas some of them had about war. On one occasion at least, this full-scale war game got out of hand. Instead of staying in the playground, it spread right through the vegetable garden tended by Don Bosco's mother. Every plant was flattened and ruined. The boys eventually stopped and were shocked at the damage that was done, but it was too late. On another occasion during a similar game, the boys destroyed the laundry area and trampled over their sheets and clothes.

Key Point

Young people are not particularly good at seeing the consequences of their actions. They can do senseless things and get into dangerous activities without thinking. That is why Don Bosco always wanted some good, friendly adult presence alongside them. He wanted the adults to show kindness to the youngsters but also to distract and guide them away from danger and towards the good, especially in the playground.

30
Finding Good in Stressed People

Don Bosco was called to hear the Confession of a man who was close to death. When he entered the sick room, the dying man fumbled under his pillow and pulled out two hand guns and pointed both at Don Bosco. "You're here because my friend persuaded me to see a priest," the man said, "but I don't believe in all that superstitious stuff so I don't want to hear the word 'Confession' or I'll shoot." The man asked him if he had come as a friend or as a priest. Don Bosco, looking at the guns said, "As a friend of course!" He then sat on the bed and talked to the man about his life, which had involved a lot of betrayals and lies. He was able to talk to Don Bosco and calm himself, make peace with his past and get ready to die. In the end Don Bosco heard his Confession and reassured him that he was loved by God and ready for heaven.

Key Point

The initial reaction from people who are frightened or hurt can be very defensive. They can be harsh in their words and behaviour towards you. Usually that is only a front. Deep down they really want to be friendly, at peace and trusting, but their history has closed their hearts and minds to goodness. Don Bosco made an act of faith that God's goodness is in all people, even the most unlikely ones.

31
Don Bosco and Great Britain

Don Bosco always wanted to come to Great Britain and work with young people. He started to learn English in Turin and was very interested when one of his friends set up a project in Cardiff. But he was even more convinced when one of his students, Dominic Savio, who later became a saint at the age of fifteen, had a dream which involved England. He saw a huge flat land covered with mist. In the mist there were many people just wandering around and lost. They were going round in circles—going nowhere. "This is England," a voice said in the dream. Then a great figure appeared carrying a flaming torch. As he raised the torch, the mist began to thin out and then disappear. The people began to look at each other, to smile and to find their way in life. As a result of this dream, Don Bosco believed that the Salesian approach to working with young people would play an important role in Great Britain at some time in the future.

Key Point

The Salesian way of working with young people can adapt to any time or culture. There is always a need for loving kindness and cheerful optimism about people. These are the things that lift the mist that separates people from one another. One of the last places that Don Bosco sent his Salesians before he died was to London. Don Bosco founded the British Province in 1887.

32
Not Being Taken In by Others—Being Shrewd

Don Bosco was walking back to his youth club in Turin when he passed a woman who was begging in the street. She had a baby bundled up in her arms and was pleading for any money she could get. Don Bosco ignored her completely and carried on walking. The boys who were with him were totally shocked. Usually Don Bosco stopped to talk to beggars and, if he had any coins, he would leave a few with them. "Why didn't you stop to give that woman some money?" they asked Don Bosco. "She has a child to feed and obviously needs help." "She has no child," said Don Bosco sharply. "Go back and look at that bundle—it's nothing but rags!" The boys ran back and looked more closely. The woman was not carrying a child and, on closer observation, she was fit and well.

Key Point

Deception and manipulation of people usually undermines the basic trust between people. It leaves one person feeling used. Honesty is always the best policy.

33
Don't Let Fear Stop You from Doing Good

In 1854 an epidemic of cholera broke out in the neighbourhood near Don Bosco's Oratory. Cholera is very infectious and a messy illness. It wiped out whole families, and people were so afraid of it that they would abandon their own families in the streets. The disease was spread through dirty water in the poorer areas of the city. Don Bosco was asked to provide help for the sick by keeping them clean and cared for in tented hospitals on the edge of the town. He asked for volunteers and 44 boys came forward. They were all taught basic hygiene techniques, and Don Bosco promised each one of them that they would not catch cholera. Not one of them caught the disease, although some did get ill through overwork, visiting the sick and working in the hospitals for long hours. This single act of volunteering meant that the city of Turin would always look favourably on the work of Don Bosco for young people.

Key Point

Risk-taking for the sake of the dignity and peace of mind of other people does not just happen when there is a cholera epidemic. We all take hidden risks when we say hello to new people in our lives, when we forgive those who have hurt us and when we offer words of praise and encouragement to our friends. Don't let fear stop you from doing a little good.

34
Putting People before Things

During the cholera epidemic the whole city began to run out of clean bandages and sheets. After a few weeks Don Bosco's mother had given all the sheets she had to the boys who were working day after day with the sick. Eventually, she had to admit that she had no more linen to give to make bandages. Then she had an idea and came back a few minutes later with three large white cloths and gave them to the boys to make more bandages. "But these are altar cloths from the chapel!" one of the boys said. "And right now I can't think of a better use for them!" Margaret replied. "People come first!"

Key Point

Putting people before things is part of Don Bosco's motto: 'Give me souls, nothing else matters' (In Latin: *Da mihi animas caetera tolle*). Salesians believe that what lasts is the love that is shared between people. We have to use things to increase the amount of loving kindness in the world.

35
Looking After Those in Need

One of Don Bosco's jobs was as chaplain to the youth offenders' prison on the edge of Turin. He visited many of the lads in there, getting to know them well and helping them when they were released. But some of them, still teenagers, were never released because they were condemned to hanging. Don Bosco had to accompany these boys to their death. He sat with one condemned teenager in his cell and heard his Confession. He promised to be there with him until the end, but he was delayed on the journey and found the boy already hanging and in the final stages of death. Don Bosco was horrified that he had not kept his promise to the boy and was shocked at the senseless violence he was seeing on the scaffold. That was the last thing he remembered. Don Bosco fainted and when he came around the boy was dead. He never attended another public hanging again. Instead, he promised himself that he would save as many lads from hanging as he could.

Key Point

Many young people run into trouble because there is no-one close by whom they can trust enough to guide them. Young people need friendly adults and good friends to help them to make good choices. When they are isolated or feel alone, they can do things that form bad habits that will eventually lead them into trouble. Good friends, family and friendly adults can prevent young people from making harmful choices—we need to be better at looking after each other.

36
Taking Risks in Trusting Others

Don Bosco visited the local young offenders' centre on a regular basis. He got to know the lads really well and felt very sorry for them. The cells were small and, in summer especially, the whole place smelt awful. They were overcrowded and often fights started just out of frustration. Don Bosco went to see the prison governor and asked if he could take them all out for the day. The governor laughed until he realised Don Bosco was serious. "They'll all run away!" he said, "And anyway, you'll have to go to a higher authority than me to get permission." Don Bosco did so and, surprisingly, was given permission, perhaps because it was hoped he might fail to bring them all back. The day, however, was a total success and all the boys returned. They all had a day in the countryside, had a few good meals and played some of the games that would have been impossible in prison. The authorities were amazed and, for the next week at least, the prison was a far happier place.

Key Point

The young prisoners all returned on time because they trusted Don Bosco and didn't want to let him down and get him into trouble. This miracle was based on a friendly approach and reminds us that all education is built on the foundation of a friendly approach and on positive relationships. It is, as Don Bosco said, "a matter of the heart."

37
Swearing

Don Bosco was travelling from a town called Ivrea back to Turin and hired a carriage for the journey. He asked if he could sit up on top with the driver, who agreed because he enjoyed a chat with his passengers. Don Bosco asked the driver if he could do him a favour. "If I can," replied the driver suspiciously. Don Bosco asked him if he could stop swearing for the length of the trip. The driver agreed it was a bad habit and he should stop. Don Bosco offered to give him ten lire[5] if he succeeded. However, after thirty yards one of the horses pulled to the right and the driver swore at it at the top of his voice. "I'll have to deduct one lira for that curse," said Don Bosco. The driver smiled and said that would be his last bit of bad language on the journey. But, when he got to Turin, the driver only had two lire left from the possible ten. "Why are bad habits so hard to break?" the driver asked. Don Bosco told him it was much easier to prevent bad habits from starting than controlling them later. He then gave him the full ten lire and asked him to keep trying.

Key Point

Don Bosco was always keen to catch bad habits before they started because he knew they could do damage. Swearing, laziness, drinking, smoking and so on can all trap people into habits that rob

---

[5] The lira (plural *lire*) was the currency of Italy until it was replaced by the euro on January 1 1999

them of their peace of mind. Sometimes, because habits can creep up on us all, we need to rely on others who might see the bad habit before we see it ourselves. So, if someone tells you that you are developing a bad habit, don't ignore them. Instead think about it—they may have done you a great favour.

38
Trusting God and
Your Own Inner Wisdom

The local baker, who supplied bread for Don Bosco's boys, thumped Don Bosco's desk. He refused to leave until he was paid in full. Don Bosco calmed him down and eventually said he would pay him that evening. He had no idea how but he had to get him out of his office. The shouting baker had attracted a few boys to the office door and Don Bosco sent them to the chapel to pray for some money to pay the baker. He needed the equivalent of £200.

Don Bosco went out for a walk—worried about the food bill from the baker. It was then that a man called out his name. He was looking for a priest to speak to his boss who was sick. Don Bosco went along, glad of the distraction. The man had been ill for a long time and he asked lots of questions about Don Bosco's work, his plans and his methods. After a while the sick man relaxed, seemingly satisfied with his talk and slipped his hand under his pillow and gave Don Bosco an envelope. Inside was the equivalent of £200—enough to pay the baker.

Key Point

When Don Bosco was in desperate need of money it eventually turned up. Sometimes what you need in your life is not given to you until just before you need it desperately. You get the courage to make new friends through loneliness. You find the courage to take responsibility at home only when there is a disaster at home. You find the calmness to manage your anger only after a lot of outbursts of temper. There is a wisdom in you that brings things out at the right time, and quiet prayer helps you to trust that wisdom. All will be well.

39
Managing Gossip

Don Bosco was in a train carriage travelling with a monk and another priest, neither of whom recognised him. They were chatting together when the monk mentioned Don Bosco. The priest almost exploded with anger. "Don't talk to me about that man!" he said. "He's a hypocrite, he says he works for the poor but lives in a big house, eats fine food and has put all his family into big houses in the countryside!" Don Bosco asked the priest if he had ever visited Don Bosco. He said he hadn't but he had heard from trusted people that this was all true. Don Bosco explained that he had been to Don Bosco's place and seen none of the things the priest had described. Don Bosco was getting off the train with the other two when someone on the platform shouted his name. The priest and the monk then realised that they had been gossiping about Don Bosco to Don Bosco himself. They were very embarrassed. The priest returned later to ask Don Bosco's forgiveness—which he readily gave.

Key Point

Very often what is true is lost in the chatter of gossip. Friendships among young people especially can be lost through believing gossip based on people being jealous or wanting to show off their insider knowledge. As far as possible, say only what you know to be true and don't make things up. By making things up and gossiping, big problems can arise and people do not trust what you say.

40
The Dangers of Loneliness

A boy called Francis at Don Bosco's school began to develop into an enthusiastic reader. Every evening until late he would read anything he could find. Eventually, friends started supplying him with cheap novels and he read more and more. He did little else. His school work began to suffer, his family hardly saw him and he barely went out of the house. Finally, his father confronted him and told him he had to change his ways, get down to work at school and help out at home. He also said that he would 'deal with him' when he got back from work that evening.

But when his father came home, Francis had gone. He had run away. The family searched for him and asked Don Bosco to look out for him but months went by with no sign. Then one day, Don Bosco saw him in the street begging for food. He gathered a few of his boys and told them to go further down the street and to catch hold of any boy that ran in their direction. Don Bosco then walked up to the boy and said, "Hello Francis." The boy looked at Don Bosco and then he ran, dropping his begging bowl in the process. Don Bosco's boys caught hold of Francis and they all went back to the Oratory. After he had been washed and reclothed, Francis recounted his story. He had worked on farms and hidden in the country but then became depressed: lonely enough and hungry enough to beg on the city streets. With great difficulty Don Bosco eventually managed to persuade Francis to return to his family, who were delighted to see him. Francis eventually settled into home life and study and qualified as a lawyer.

Key Point

Being alone is important for everyone. We all need space for ourselves. But it is unhealthy to be always alone and avoiding other people. If that happens, you can get very low in spirits. Having a few good people to talk to at home or at school gives you the energy to get through worries. Shared sports, hobbies and conversations can be a great source of strength as you grow up.

41
Assassination—Dealing with Violence

Don Bosco was teaching a class in the choir loft of the church. He was just pointing to one of the boys when a shot rang out. It was deafening, and at the same time the plaster on the wall behind Don Bosco exploded. It took a few minutes to realise what had happened. Someone had tried to shoot Don Bosco! Then one of the boys pointed to Don Bosco's cassock—the black robe worn by priests at that time. There was a hole in it just under the armpit close to his heart. Don Bosco seemed to stay very calm. "Maybe God nudged the assassin's elbow at the last minute!" he joked.

The man who carried out the shooting was caught soon afterwards; he was a well-known criminal and had been seen running away. He admitted that he had been paid well to assassinate Don Bosco. However, he escaped jail completely because the people who paid him were part of an underground group that had a lot of influence with the police and the judges. Later, Don Bosco met the man in the street and asked him why he had tried to shoot him. "For the money, Don Bosco," he replied, "It was nothing personal." Don Bosco called him an unhappy man, someone who had been manipulated by others who were too cowardly to challenge Don Bosco face-to-face.

Key Point

There are people around us who have money or influence to get us to do things we would later regret. We can be pushed around by others to do things that are wrong because we want to be popular with them. If someone asks you to do something that you know is wrong, tell them to do it themselves and take the consequences. Otherwise you may end up hurting people and becoming a bully yourself. Like Don Bosco, keep calm and just say a firm "no" to what is wrong.

42
Managing Bullies

Don Bosco was a great writer and produced a regular magazine called 'Catholic Readings' ('*Letture Cattoliche*'). Some groups in the town were not happy because it was growing in circulation and strengthening the spiritual lives of ordinary people. These groups wanted to get rid of the magazine. Don Bosco was visited in his office in the youth centre by two representatives of the groups, who began by complimenting him on the quality of the printing and the layout of the magazine. Then they said that it was a shame about all the religious content he was putting in. They suggested he stick to arts, sports and science instead. To make their point, they took out a lot of money and put it on the desk in front of Don Bosco as an advance for changing the magazine content.

When Don Bosco refused both the request and the money, the visitors stood up and said that they were insulted by his refusal. One of them said that he should be very afraid to walk the streets after such a refusal and he had better prepare to die. Don Bosco just smiled and said, "Threatening a Catholic priest on something like this is a total waste of time. If we have to die for what we believe, we will do that readily. Besides, these kinds of threats only make you look ridiculous." The two callers lost their temper at that point and tried to attack Don Bosco; however, when the door opened and two of Don Bosco's students came into the room, they quickly changed their minds and left.

Key Point

Anyone who makes threats to force another person to do something wrong usually ends up looking ridiculous. Deep down they know they are in the wrong but are just not going to admit it even to themselves. Resisting these threats builds up your inner strength and dignity and can often shame the other person into backing off.

43
Don Bosco and Poisoning— Keeping Doing Good

Don Bosco was called out to visit a sick person late at night. He lived in a violent area of the city and most other priests would not go there at night, so Don Bosco was often called instead. For that reason, Don Bosco used to take three or four older boys with him. On this occasion they were needed.

He was led by a relative of the sick person to a building, the ground floor of which was a pub. He had to go through the pub to reach the stairs to the rooms where the sick person was waiting. As he walked through the pub four men got up and blocked his way. "Have a drink Don Bosco," they said, holding out a glass for him. When Don Bosco refused, they got angry. They tried to grab his arms and force the drink—almost certainly poisoned—down his throat. Fortunately, Don Bosco was strong and forced them away, but he only made it to the door of the pub before they caught him again. However, the noise had alerted Don Bosco's lads outside, all of whom were strong and well-built builders' apprentices, and they came into the pub, surrounded Don Bosco and escorted him out. The other men, with plenty of alcohol in them, were no match for those lads. The whole affair had been a trick to poison Don Bosco and discredit his reputation.

Key Point

When a person does good and helps others, most people are happy and ready to support them. But not all. When you do good there will always be someone who will try to test your goodness and to make you suffer in some way. They will tell lies, turn people against you and undermine your goodness. In order to keep doing good you need two things: trusted friends who will support you and a strong friendship with God through prayer. If you have those two things, your goodness will survive.

44
A Knife Attack— Avoiding Revenge

Don Bosco always believed that his Oratory was a safe place, but one day a man broke in waving a large knife and swearing to kill Don Bosco. The boys ran away from him and the man spotted a priest and chased him around the playground until he realised it wasn't Don Bosco. Don Bosco appeared on his balcony over the playground to see his boys cornering the man. They were armed with sticks and large stones. Don Bosco persuaded them to put them down and back off. Someone called for the police, but they took over an hour to arrive before the man was arrested and taken away.

The police returned a few hours later and asked if he wanted to press charges. "As a Christian I am ready to forgive him," Don Bosco replied, "but as a citizen I need to protect my youth centre and the boys in it, so I will prosecute him."

Key Point

If we resort to violence, we become like animals. If the boys had injured or even killed that assassin, the work of the youth centre would have been damaged and some boys could have been tried for murder. As good citizens and honest Christians, we are obliged to follow the rule of law and not take the law into our own hands. Revenge and hatred do not make a good foundation for community or for a school.

45
Realising Your Mistakes—
Being Hopeful

One of Don Bosco's past pupils came to visit him. Once in Don Bosco's office he began to weep like a child. He was a grown man by now and Don Bosco thought he might have mental health problems. Instead, he looked at Don Bosco with a tear-stained face and said that he had been sent there to kill him! He then said that as soon as he had seen Don Bosco again, he remembered his kindness for him as a young orphan. He admitted that he couldn't shoot Don Bosco and took the gun out of his coat pocket and threw it onto the floor. He told Don Bosco that he was part of a gang that was being paid to murder him and, through drawing lots, he had been chosen to do the deed.

Both Don Bosco and the past pupil knew that the gang would now want to kill their gang member for disobeying their orders. The poor young man ran away and later tried to drown himself in the river nearby. He was brought back to Don Bosco and was kept safe until later that month when Don Bosco got him out of the country to start a new life.

Key Point

It is easy to find yourself caught up in groups and gangs that eventually persuade you to do things that normally you would never even think of. Usually it leads to shame if you do the things they want or fear if you don't. These groups and gangs slowly take over your mind and rob you of your freedom. The only way forward is to trust someone else outside the gang or the group and work towards breaking your connection with them. Your real life, the best you that you can become, belongs elsewhere.

46
Needing Others—The Limits of Independence

Turin in the 1850s was a chaotic and growing city: being out at night was dangerous. There were few street lights and a large number of violent characters on the streets. Don Bosco's mother was always afraid when he had to go out to meetings and sick calls after dark. She was proved right one night when Don Bosco was walking back from a meeting in the city. He suddenly heard movement behind him in the dark and glimpsed a man running at him with a knife. Don Bosco ran, but ahead of him three other men stepped across the street and blocked his escape. Don Bosco turned to meet the man with the knife and surprised him with a punch to his arm that knocked the knife out of his hand, then he added another punch into his stomach that brought his assailant to the ground.

The other three men closed the distance on Don Bosco but never laid a hand on him because at that moment a huge grey dog appeared out of nowhere and hit the leading man in the chest, knocking him to the floor. The other two, seeing the fierce teeth and the size of the dog, ran off with the dog chasing them. Don Bosco got hold of the man who had tried to stab him, and the dog appeared at his side as the remaining men all ran away. From then on this dog always appeared at night when Don Bosco had to go out. Some nights it stopped Don Bosco leaving home completely.

It stood about a metre high, was similar to an Irish Wolfhound and was a dark grey colour. Don Bosco called it '*Grigio*', which means 'grey' in Italian.

Key Point

We all like to feel that we are independent, making our own decisions and making our own way in life. Grigio reminds us that we all need support in some way. We need family, friendships, good advice and good listeners if we are to stay safe and grow in wisdom. Who is your Grigio—the one who keeps you out of trouble and is never far away when you need them?

47
Being Assertive with Aggressive People

One day when Don Bosco was away for a few hours, some government inspectors arrived without warning wanting to see all the records of the youth centre and the school. They were met by Don Bosco's administrator, Don Alasonatti, who was a quiet and frail priest who worked in the office. The two inspectors asked for all sorts of statistics, demanded to see the accounts and asked further questions accusing Don Alasonatti of lying. The poor priest was terrified of their anger and accusations and eventually he collapsed on the floor. It was then that Don Bosco returned.

"I hope you are both proud of yourselves," he said to the men. "You have come here with armed guards to frighten us and to find if we were doing anything against the government. So why don't you ask me and not torture someone else with questions they can't answer?" These men were bullies and Don Bosco was not going to be intimidated by them. He faced up to them and they backed down when they discovered he had nothing to hide except unpaid bills for food.

Key Point

The officials came with a search warrant at a time when Don Bosco was away so that they could intimidate some of the staff. As soon as Don Bosco arrived, they gave up because he would not be pushed around by them even if he was frightened by their soldiers and guns. Standing up to bullies does not mean physically fighting them; it means refusing to be pressurised by their angry presence. Keeping calm, remembering God's presence and your own goodness will always help to get you through these challenges.

48
The Death of a Parent— Managing Loss

Don Bosco's mother, Margaret, worked for many years in Don Bosco's youth centre and provided food and clothing for over 300 boarders, many of whom were homeless. She eventually fell ill and retired to bed with pneumonia. It was clear to all that she was dying when she called Don Bosco to her room for a final conversation. Margaret spent a lot of that conversation talking about the family spirit of the centre and identified the people he could trust to maintain that family spirit in her absence. She rapidly grew worse and Don Bosco's brother, Joseph, arrived to be with her.

As she got close to the end of her illness, Margaret asked Don Bosco to leave the room. It was too painful for him to watch her dying and she found his pain too much to bear. So she died with her son Joseph by her side and Don Bosco waiting in his own room for the news. When they cleared her room after the funeral they found nothing in the drawers and cupboards. She had given away everything that she owned.

Key Point

Margaret decided to work for young people and bit by bit gave away everything for that purpose. She had nothing left in material possessions but had a rich story of loving kindness to her name.

She had raised a family single-handedly, taught her boys to be honest and strong, created a family spirit in the youth centre and learnt to trust God and to trust life. We too need to let go of things that only give short-term pleasure and build up treasure in heaven where only loving kindness survives. Only what is done in love lasts.

49
Building Friendships across Cultures

John Bosco went to school in a town called Chieri where there was a small Jewish area. The Jewish people were tolerated in the town but regarded as a bit strange and as second-class citizens. John Bosco was sixteen years of age when he made friends with one of them called Jonah, with whom he got on really well. They were both into music and were great storytellers. On Saturday Jonah would not come into school because it is a holy day for Jews, and John would take notes and even complete homework for him so that he didn't get into trouble. This was a real and lasting friendship for both boys despite the cultural differences involved.

However, when Jonah's mother saw this friendship developing, she became angry and confronted John. "Why are you interested in Jonah? Are you trying to convert him to Christianity?" she asked furiously. John tried to argue that they just got on well together and that was it. Jonah's family did not trust the friendship and moved him away. Later, when Jonah was older, he came back to the area and finally did become a Christian. He remained a friend to Don Bosco throughout his life.

Key Point

Friendships that are good and healthy will last, even if there are times of misunderstanding and separation. We all need to give time to friends but also leave them free to be themselves with their own culture and personality. It is easy to start manipulating and pressurising friends in a way that is not healthy. Good, healthy friendships are open, honest, kind and cheerful. How are your friendships at home and at school?

50
Having Compassion for Others

Don Bosco was ordered by his doctor to leave Turin and return to his family home for a few weeks' rest. He was told to take a donkey and not to walk as he was not well enough. Once home, he walked a little each day and began to get stronger. By week three he was strong enough to walk to a town called Capriglio—the place where his mother was born. As he walked the dusty road, he heard rustling in the hedge and a voice rang out: "Your money or your life!" Speaking into the hedge, Don Bosco said that he had no money. Then he saw the man's face and, despite a rough beard, recognised it instantly. "Cortese!" Don Bosco exclaimed, "What are you doing here, trying to rob people?"

He was one of the prisoners that Don Bosco had worked with in Turin, and now he was embarrassed to have been recognised so far from home. As they walked, Don Bosco listened to his story about his family rejecting him when he went to prison and the impossibility of finding any work. When they reached his mother's house, Don Bosco invited him in for a meal and a place to stay overnight. In the morning he wrote a reference for him and gave him the name of some employers in Turin who would give a second chance to ex-prisoners.

Key Point

You can get away with being dishonest for a while but eventually the truth comes out. Once you get a reputation for dishonesty, few people will take the risk of trusting you again. So honesty is always your best policy. But as Christians we are encouraged to give people a second chance, an opportunity to change, so that they can become a better person. That is what Don Bosco did. Who might need forgiveness and a second chance from you?

51
Asking for What You Need

Don Bosco had to spend a lot of time fundraising to feed the homeless lads in his youth centre. In that task he was not afraid to approach anyone to ask for money for food and clothing. On one visit to a wealthy lady in Turin he was shown by a maid into a very expensive room to wait. When the lady of the house came into the room, she was shocked. Don Bosco had rolled back the expensive Persian carpet and was standing on the cold tiles underneath.

"What do you think you are doing?" the lady demanded. "Well," said Don Bosco, "I am such a poor priest and this carpet is so very expensive that I felt I couldn't stand on it." The lady looked at him strangely and then laughed. He had made his point: he was poor and she was rich. He needed money to feed his boys and she had money to spend on Persian carpets. Don Bosco walked out with the value of the carpet in money, and his boys ate well for the next month.

Key Point

You will get much further with a cheerful and humorous approach than with a miserable and critical approach. St Francis de Sales, Don Bosco's patron, said the same: "You will attract more bees with a spoonful of honey than with a barrel full of vinegar." Kindness and good humour are better in getting what you need from others than misery and moaning.

52
Don't Make Threats You Can't Keep

In the dining room at Don Bosco's youth centre there was always a lot of high spirits. Noise levels were equally high. The teacher on duty was having great difficulty stopping some of the boys throwing food at each other. Eventually, he quietened them down and told them off. He was angry with them and it showed. He said that the next boy to throw food would be expelled. He felt that would shock them into behaving but it didn't. One of the boys was caught throwing food because it hit the teacher in the face. All the boys laughed but he knew who had thrown it. He called his name, sent him out and later took him to Don Bosco. The teacher left the boy outside Don Bosco's office and went in and explained what had happened and how he had promised that he would be expelled. Don Bosco listened and then called the boy into his office.

The boy was immediately expelled and sent home. The teacher was surprised and upset; he hadn't meant that to happen. Don Bosco called the teacher in later and said, "If you say something to the boys from a position of authority, I will support you because we work as a team. If you make threats, they have to be carried out or you will lose all authority in school. But you were wrong. A food fight is not a cause for expelling a boy. It is out of proportion to the fault. I suspect that you did it out of anger and that is never a good reason to make a threat. Try to have a quiet word, especially when thoughtlessness is involved." The teacher left Don Bosco ashamed, and Don Bosco readmitted the boy about six months later.

Key Point

If a young person is punished, then the punishment needs to be proportional to the fault as it is seen by the young person. It should never be in proportion to the anger that the teacher might legitimately feel.

DON BOSCO'S ADVICE ON WORK WITH THE YOUNG

St John Bosco was an educator of young people in the city of Turin during the Industrial Revolution. Dealing with homeless and often damaged adolescents led to his development of a preventive system. This was based on a reasonable, affectionate and spiritual approach to the young. His approach worked with most young people and also helped the teachers to work with heartfelt realism for the good of young people. Here are a few of his thoughts on working with the young.

If I want to be a true parent to these children, then I must have a parent's heart and not turn to repression or to punishment without reason and without justice.

It is certainly easier to lose one's temper than to be patient, threaten young people rather than reason with them. It often suits our lack of patience and our pride to punish those who resist us, rather than bear with them firmly and with kindness.

Correction should be done in private and in an atmosphere of care for the individual. Never rebuke anyone in public except to prevent a scandal or to correct a scandal if it has already occurred.

I have rarely seen any advantage gained from improvised punishments inflicted before other means were tried.

Adults do not always adopt the best approach in their dealings with young people. Either they hand out standardised punishments and achieve nothing, or they just strike out, rightly or wrongly. This is the reason why we often see disruption multiply and discontent spread even among the better children.

If young people are already ruined at such an early age, it is due more to carelessness than to any ingrained malice. These young people have a need for some kind person to show care, to work with them and guide them in virtues.

Let it be seen that no other rules are required than those that are absolutely reasonable and necessary.

Look for someone to whom the child can open up his trouble, in a way that perhaps he cannot do with you because he is not sure that he will be believed or because he is too proud to admit that he should.

When you have won over a stubborn spirit in a child I beg you not only to leave him the hope of being forgiven by you but, through good behaviour, to cancel even the memory of his mistakes.

To forget and to cause to be forgotten the unhappy days of a young person's mistakes is the supreme art of a good educator.

You can get further with a friendly look, with a word of encouragement that gives new heart and courage than with repeated blame which serves only to upset and diminish enthusiasm.

Adults should try to avoid like the plague every kind of morbid affection or favouritism with young people. They should realise that the wrong doing of any one adult can compromise the whole situation.

Teachers should precede pupils to their class; they should remain with them until another teacher comes; they should never allow young people to be idle.

I have often noted that adults who demand silence hand out punishments easily, and who exacted prompt and blind obedience were invariably the ones who showed little respect for the useful advice that I and other colleagues found it necessary to give.

Teachers who never forgive their pupils are often in the habit of forgiving themselves everything.

Whenever there is a need to punish, great prudence is required. First of all, wait until you are in control of yourself; do not let it be understood that you are acting because of a bad mood or in anger. In this event you put your own authority at risk and the punishment would become harmful.

Even the young realise that it is only reason that has the right to correct them.

Do not punish anyone the moment that the fault has been committed, for fear that they may not be able to own up or to overcome their emotions and recognise the need for the punishment. Otherwise they may become even more embittered and commit the same or even worse faults. You need to give them time to recover, think things over and to acknowledge their mistakes. At the same time, they are more likely to see the justice of the penalty imposed and so profit by the experience.

Why do people want to replace loving kindness with cold rules?

When adults are thought of as superior and no longer as a parental figure or a friend, they are feared and little loved. And so, if you want to be of one heart and mind, for the love of God, you must break down this fatal barrier of mistrust and replace it with a spirit of confidence. How do you break through this barrier? By a friendly and an informal approach with the young, especially in play and free time. You cannot have loving kindness without this familiarity, and where it is not evident there can be no confidence. If you want to be loved, you must make it clear that you love.

The more you act from spite, the less you will be listened to.

Let us rid ourselves of all anger when we have to curb young people's faults. No commotion of spirit, no scornful looks, no hurtful words on our lips. Instead, let us feel compassion for what is happening and offer hope for the future.

Let us remember that force punishes the offence but does not heal the offender. One does not cultivate a plant by harsh violence and so one does not educate the young person's will by burdening it with a yoke that is too heavy to bear.

Do not use expressions calculated to humiliate. Express hope and the readiness to forgive when the behaviour improves.

The teacher who is seen only in the classroom remains just another teacher and nothing more; but if they appear in recreation they become a friend. How many changes of heart have been achieved because of a quiet word in the ear whilst a young person is in recreation!

Someone who knows that they are loved will love in return, and one who loves can obtain anything, especially from the young.

Confidence creates an electric current between youngsters and their teachers. Hearts are opened, needs and weaknesses made known. This confidence enables the teacher to put up with the weariness, annoyance, the ingratitude and the troubles that young people cause. Jesus did not crush the bruised reed nor quench the wavering candle. He is your model. When this confidence and loving kindness fails nothing will go well.

Remember that education is largely a matter of the heart. God is the master educator and we will be unable to achieve any lasting good unless God teaches us the art of education and puts the key into our hands.

The heart of a young person is like a fortress which is always closed to rigour and harshness. Let us strive to make ourselves loved, to inculcate a sense of duty and a fear of doing wrong. Then we will see the doors of many hearts open with great ease.

OTHER BOOKS BY DAVID O'MALLEY

A Salesian Way of life

Advent and Christmas Swatch

Christian Leadership

Ordinary Ways

Prayers to Start My Day

Prayers to Close my Day

School Ethos and Chaplaincy

Swatch and Pray (with Tonino Passerello)

Swatch Journey through Lent

The Christian Teacher

Walking with Don Bosco

Available from:
Don Bosco Publications
Thornleigh House
Sharples Park
Bolton
BL1 6PQ

01204 308811
publications@salesians.org.uk
www.salesians.org.uk